The Essays of Anthony Trollope

Index of Contents

How To Ride To Hounds

Now attend me, Diana and the Nymphs, Pan, Orion, and the Satyrs, for I have a task in hand which may hardly be accomplished without some divine aid. And the lesson I would teach is one as to which even gods must differ, and no two men will ever hold exactly the same opinion. Indeed, no written lesson, no spoken words, no lectures, be they ever so often repeated, will teach any man to ride to hounds. The art must come of nature and of experience; and Orion, were he here, could only tell the tyro of some few blunders which he may avoid, or give him a hint or two as to the manner in which he should begin.

Let it be understood that I am speaking of fox-hunting, and let the young beginner always remember that in hunting the fox a pack of hounds is needed. The huntsman, with his servants, and all the scarlet-coated horsemen in the field, can do nothing towards the end for which they are assembled without hounds. He who as yet knows nothing of hunting will imagine that I am laughing at him in saying this; but, after a while, he will know how needful it is to bear in mind the caution I here give him, and will see how frequently men seem to forget that a fox cannot be hunted without hounds. A fox is seen to break from the covert, and men ride after it; the first man, probably, being some cunning sinner, who would fain get off alone if it were possible, and steal a march upon the field. But in this case one knave makes many fools; and men will rush, and ride along the track of the game, as though they could hunt it, and will destroy the scent before the hounds are on it, following, in their ignorance, the footsteps of the cunning sinner. Let me beg my young friend not to be found among this odious crowd of marplots. His business is to ride to hounds; and let him do so from the beginning of the run, persevering through it all, taking no mean advantages, and allowing himself to be betrayed into as few mistakes as possible; but let him not begin before the beginning. If he could know all that is inside the breast of that mean man who commenced the scurry, the cunning man who desires to steal a march, my young friend would not wish to emulate him. With nine-tenths of the men who flutter away after this ill fashion there is no design of their own in their so riding. They simply wish to get away, and in their impatience forget the little fact that a pack of hounds is necessary for the hunting of a fox.

I have found myself compelled to begin with this preliminary caution, as all riding to hounds hangs on the fact in question. Men cannot ride to hounds if the hounds be not there. They may ride one after another, and that, indeed, suffices for many a keen sportsman; but I am now addressing the youth who is ambitious of riding to hounds. But though I have thus begun, striking first at the very root of the matter, I must go back with my pupil into the covert before I carry him on through the run. In riding to hounds there is much to do before the straight work commences. Indeed, the straight work is, for the man, the easiest work, or the work, I should say, which may be done with the least previous knowledge. Then the horse, with his qualities, comes into play; and if he be up to his business in skill, condition, and bottom, a man may go well by simply keeping with others who go well also. Straight riding, however, is the exception and not the rule. It comes sometimes, and is the cream of hunting when it does come; but it does not come as often as the enthusiastic beginner will have taught himself to expect.

But now we will go back to the covert, and into the covert if it be a large one. I will speak of three kinds of coverts, the gorse, the wood, and the forest. There are others, but none other so distinct as to require reference. As regards the gorse covert, which of all is the most delightful, you, my disciple, need only be careful to keep in the crowd when it is being drawn. You must understand that if the plantation which you see before you, and which is the fox's home and homestead, be surrounded, the owner of it will never leave it. A fox will run back from a child among a pack of hounds, so much more terrible is to him the human race even than the canine. The object of all men of course is that the fox shall go, and from a gorse covert of five acres he must go very quickly or die among the hounds. It will not be long before he starts if there be space left for him to creep out, as he will hope, unobserved. Unobserved he will not be, for the accustomed eye of some whip or servant will have seen him from a corner. But if stray horsemen roaming round the gorse give him no room for such hope, he will not go. All which is so plainly intelligible, that you, my friend, will not fail to understand why you are required to remain with the crowd. And with simple gorse coverts there is no strong temptation to move about. They are drawn quickly, and though there be a scramble for places when the fox has broken, the whole thing is in so small a compass that there is no difficulty in getting away with the hounds. In finding your right place, and keeping it when it is found, you may have difficulty; but in going away from a gorse the field will be open for you, and when the hounds are well out and upon the scent, then remember your Latin; Occupet extremum scabies.

But for one fox found in a gorse you will, in ordinary countries, see five found in woods; and as to the place and conduct of a hunting man while woods are being drawn, there is room for much doubt. I presume that you intend to ride one horse throughout the day, and that you wish to see all the hunting that may come in your way. This being so, it will be your study to economize your animal's power, and to keep him fresh for the run when it comes. You will hardly assist your object in this respect by seeing the wood drawn, and galloping up and down the rides as the fox crosses and recrosses from one side of it to another. Such rides are deep with mud, and become deeper as the work goes on; and foxes are very obstinate, running, if the covert be thick, often for an hour together without an attempt at breaking, and being driven back when they do attempt by the horsemen whom they see on all sides of them. It is very possible to continue at this work, seeing the hounds hunt, with your ears rather than your eyes, till your nag has nearly done his day's work. He will still carry you perhaps throughout a good run, but he will not do so with that elasticity which you will love; and then, after that, the journey home is, it is occasionally something almost too frightful to be contemplated. You can, therefore, if it so please you, station yourself with other patient long-suffering, mindful men at some corner, or at some central point amidst the rides, biding your time, consoling yourself with cigars, and not swearing at the vile perfidious, unfoxlike fox more frequently than you can help. For the fox on such occasions will be abused with all the calumnious epithets which the ingenuity of angry men can devise, because he is exercising that ingenuity the possession of which on his part is the foundation of fox-hunting. There you will remain, nursing your horse, listening to chaff, and hoping. But even when the fox does go, your difficulties may be but beginning.

It is possible he may have gone on your side of the wood; but much more probable that he should have taken the other. He loves not that crowd that has been abusing him, and steals away from some silent distant corner. You, who are a beginner, hear nothing of his going; and when you rush off, as you will do with others, you will hardly know at first why the rush is made. But some one with older eyes and more experienced ears has seen signs and heard sounds, and knows that the fox is away. Then, my friend, you have your place to win, and it may be that the distance shall be too great to allow of your winning it. Nothing but experience will guide you safely through these difficulties.

In drawing forests or woodlands your course is much clearer. There is no question, then, of standing still and waiting with patience, tobacco, and chaff for the coming start. The area to be drawn is too large to admit of waiting, and your only duty is to stay as close to the hounds as your ears and eyes will permit, remembering always that your ears should serve you much more often than your eyes. And in woodland hunting that which you thus see and hear is likely to be your amusement for the day. There is "ample room and verge enough" to run a fox down without any visit to the open country, and by degrees, as a true love of hunting comes upon you in place of a love of riding, you will learn to think that a day among the woodlands is a day not badly spent. At first, when after an hour and a half the fox has been hunted to his death, or has succeeded in finding some friendly hole, you will be wondering when the fun is going to begin. Ah me! how often have I gone through all the fun, have seen the fun finished, and then have wondered when it was going to begin; and that, too, in other things besides hunting!

But at present the fun shall not be finished, and we will go back to the wood from which the fox is just breaking. You, my pupil, shall have been patient, and your patience shall be rewarded by a good start. On the present occasion I will give you the exquisite delight of knowing that you are there, at the spot, as the hounds come out of the covert. Your success, or want of success, throughout the run will depend on the way in which you may now select to go over the three or four first fields. It is not difficult to keep with hounds if you can get well away with them, and be with them when they settle to their running. In a long and fast run your horse may, of course, fail you. That must depend on his power and his condition. But, presuming your horse to be able to go, keeping with hounds is not difficult when you are once free from the thick throng of the riders. And that thick throng soon makes itself thin. The difficulty is in the start, and you will almost be offended when I suggest to you what those difficulties are, and suggest also that such as they are even they may overcome you. You have to choose your line of riding. Do not let your horse choose it for you instead of choosing it for yourself. He will probably make such attempts, and it is not at all improbable that you should let him have his way. Your horse will be as anxious to go as you are, but his anxiety will carry him after some other special horse on which he has fixed his eyes. The rider of that horse may not be the guide that you would select. But some human guide you must select. Not at first will you, not at first does any man, choose for himself with serene precision of confident judgment the line which he will take. You will be flurried, anxious, self-diffident, conscious of your own ignorance, and desirous of a leader. Many of those men who are with you will have objects at heart very different from your object. Some will ride for certain points, thinking that they can foretell the run of the fox. They may be right; but you, in your new ambition, are not solicitous to ride away to some other covert because the fox may, perchance, be going there. Some are thinking of the roads. Others are remembering that brook which is before them, and riding wide for a ford. With none such, as I presume, do you wish to place yourself. Let the hounds be your mark; and if, as may often be the case, you cannot see them, then see the huntsman; or, if you cannot see him, follow, at any rate, some one who does. If you can even do this as a beginner, you will not do badly.

But, whenever it be possible, let the hounds themselves be your mark, and endeavour to remember that the leading hounds are those which should guide you. A single hound who turns when he is heading the pack should teach you to turn also. Of all the hounds you see there in the open, probably not one-third are hunting. The others are doing as you do, following where their guides lead them. It is for you to follow the real guide, and not the followers, if only you can keep the real guide in view. To keep the whole pack in view and to ride among them is easy enough when the scent is slack and the pace is slow. At such times let me counsel you to retire somewhat from the crowd, giving place to those eager men who are breaking the huntsman's heart. When the hounds have come nearer to their fox, and the pace is again good, then they will retire and make room for you.

Not behind hounds, but alongside of them, if only you can achieve such position, it should be your honour and glory to place yourself; and you should go so far wide of them as in no way to impede them or disturb them, or even to remind them of your presence. If thus you live with them, turning as they turn, but never turning among them, keeping your distance, but losing no yard, and can do this for seven miles over a grass country in forty-five minutes, then you can ride to hounds better than nineteen men out of every twenty that you have seen at the meet, and will have enjoyed the keenest pleasure that hunting, or perhaps, I may say, that any other amusement, can give you.

The Hunting Farmer

Few hunting men calculate how much they owe to the hunting farmer, or recognize the fact that hunting farmers contribute more than any other class of sportsmen towards the maintenance of the sport. It is hardly too much to say that hunting would be impossible if farmers did not hunt. If they were inimical to hunting, and men so closely concerned must be friends or enemies, there would be no foxes left alive; and no fox, if alive, could be kept above ground. Fences would be impracticable, and damages would be ruinous; and any attempt to maintain the institution of hunting would be a long warfare in which the opposing farmer would certainly be the ultimate conqueror. What right has the hunting man who goes down from London, or across from Manchester, to ride over the ground which he treats as if it were his own, and to which he thinks that free access is his undoubted privilege? Few men, I fancy, reflect that they have no such right, and no such privilege, or recollect that the very scene and area of their exercise, the land that makes hunting possible to them, is contributed by the farmer. Let any one remember with what tenacity the exclusive right of entering upon their small territories is clutched and maintained by all cultivators in other countries; let him remember the enclosures of France, the vine and olive terraces of Tuscany, or the narrowly-watched fields of Lombardy; the little meadows of Switzerland on which no stranger's foot is allowed to come, or the Dutch pastures, divided by dykes, and made safe from all intrusions. Let him talk to the American farmer of English hunting, and explain to that independent, but somewhat prosaic husbandman, that in England two or three hundred men claim the right of access to every man's land during the whole period of the winter months! Then, when he thinks of this, will he realize to himself what it is that the English farmer contributes to hunting in England? The French countryman cannot be made to understand it. You cannot induce him to believe that if he held land in England, looking to make his rent from tender young grass-fields and patches of sprouting corn, he would be powerless to keep out intruders, if those intruders came in the shape of a rushing squadron of cavalry, and called themselves a hunt. To him, in accordance with his existing ideas, rural life under such circumstances would be impossible. A small pan of charcoal, and an honourable death-bed, would give him relief after his first experience of such an invasion.

Nor would the English farmer put up with the invasion, if the English farmer were not himself a hunting man. Many farmers, doubtless, do not hunt, and they bear it, with more or less grace; but they are inured to it from their infancy, because it is in accordance with the habits and pleasures of their own race. Now and again, in every hunt, some man comes up, who is, indeed, more frequently a small proprietor new to the glories of ownership, than a tenant farmer, who determines to vindicate his rights and oppose the field. He puts up a wire-fence round his domain, thus fortifying himself, as it were, in his citadel, and defies the world around him. It is wonderful how great is the annoyance which one such man may give, and how thoroughly he may destroy the comfort of the coverts in his neighbourhood. But, strong as such an one is in his fortress, there are still the means of fighting him. The farmers around him, if they be hunting men, make the place too hot to hold him. To them he is a thing accursed, a man to be spoken of with all evil language, as one who desires to get more out of his land than Providence, that is, than an English Providence, has intended. Their own wheat is exposed, and it is abominable to them that the wheat of another man should be more sacred than theirs.

All this is not sufficiently remembered by some of us when the period of the year comes which is trying to the farmer's heart, when the young clover is growing, and the barley has been just sown. Farmers, as a rule, do not think very much of their wheat. When such riding is practicable, of course they like to see men take the headlands and furrows; but their hearts are not broken by the tracks of horses across their wheat-fields. I doubt, indeed, whether wheat is ever much injured by such usage. But let the thoughtful rider avoid the new-sown barley; and, above all things, let him give a wide berth to the new-laid meadows of artificial grasses. They are never large, and may always be shunned. To them the poaching of numerous horses is absolute destruction. The surface of such enclosures should be as smooth as a billiard-table, so that no water may lie in holes; and, moreover, any young plant cut by a horse's foot is trodden out of existence. Farmers do see even this done, and live through it without open warfare; but they should not be put to such trials of temper or pocket too often.

And now for my friend the hunting farmer in person, the sportsman whom I always regard as the most indispensable adjunct to the field, to whom I tender my spare cigar with the most perfect expression of my good will. His dress is nearly always the same. He wears a thick black coat, dark brown breeches, and top boots, very white in colour, or of a very dark mahogany, according to his taste. The hunting farmer of the old school generally rides in a chimney-pot hat; but, in this particular, the younger brethren of the plough are leaving their old habits, and running into caps, net hats, and other innovations which, I own, are somewhat distasteful to me. And there is, too, the ostentatious farmer, who rides in scarlet, signifying thereby that he subscribes his ten or fifteen guineas to the hunt fund. But here, in this paper, it is not of him I speak. He is a man who is so much less the farmer, in that he is the more an ordinary man of the ordinary world. The farmer whom we have now before us shall wear the old black coat, and the old black hat, and the white top boots, rather daubed in their whiteness; and he shall be the genuine farmer of the old school.

My friend is generally a modest man in the field, seldom much given to talking unless he be first addressed; and then he prefers that you shall take upon yourself the chief burden of the conversation. But on certain hunting subjects he has his opinion, indeed, a very strong opinion, and if you can drive him from that, your eloquence must be very great. He is very urgent about special coverts, and even as to special foxes; and you will often find smouldering in his bosom, if you dive deep enough to search for it, a half-smothered fire of indignation against the master because the country has, according to our friend's views, been drawn amiss. In such matters the farmer is generally right; but he is slow to communicate his ideas, and does not recognize the fact that other men have not the same opportunities for observation which belong to him. A master, however, who understands his business will generally consult a farmer; and he will seldom, I think, or perhaps never, consult any one else.

Always shake hands with your friend the farmer. It puts him at his ease with you, and he will tell you more willingly after that ceremony what are his ideas about the wind, and what may be expected of the day. His day's hunting is to him a solemn thing, and he gives to it all his serious thought. If any man can predicate anything of the run of a fox, it is the farmer.

I had almost said that if any one knew anything of scent, it is the farmer; but of scent I believe that not even the farmer knows anything. But he knows very much as to the lie of the country, and should my gentle reader by chance have taken a glass or two of wine above ordinary over night, the effect of which will possibly be a temporary distaste to straight riding, no one's knowledge as to the line of the lanes is so serviceable as that of the farmer.

As to riding, there is the ambitious farmer and the unambitious farmer; the farmer who rides hard, that is, ostensibly hard, and the farmer who is simply content to know where the hounds are, and to follow them at a distance which shall maintain him in that knowledge. The ambitious farmer is not the hunting farmer in his normal condition; he is either one who has an eye to selling his horse, and, riding with that view, loses for the time his position as farmer; or he is some exceptional tiller of the soil who probably is dangerously addicted to hunting as another man is addicted to drinking; and you may surmise respecting him that things will not go well with him after a year or two. The friend of my heart is the farmer who rides, but rides without sputtering; who never makes a show of it, but still is always there; who feels it to be no disgrace to avoid a run of fences when his knowledge tells him that this may be done without danger of his losing his place. Such an one always sees a run to the end. Let the pace have been what it may, he is up in time to see the crowd of hounds hustling for their prey, and to take part in the buzz of satisfaction which the prosperity of the run has occasioned. But the farmer never kills his horse, and seldom rides him even to distress. He is not to be seen loosing his girths, or looking at the beast's flanks, or examining his legs to ascertain what mischances may have occurred. He takes it all easily, as men always take matters of business in which they are quite at home. At the end of the run he sits mounted as quietly as he did at the meet, and has none of that appearance of having done something wonderful, which on such occasions is so very strong in the faces of the younger portion of the pink brigade. To the farmer his day's hunting is very pleasant, and by habit is even very necessary; but it comes in its turn like market-day, and produces no extraordinary excitement. He does not rejoice over an hour and ten minutes with a kill in the open, as he rejoices when he has returned to Parliament the candidate who is pledged to repeal of the malt-tax; for the farmer of whom we are speaking now, though he rides with constancy, does not ride with enthusiasm.

O fortunati sua si bona norint farmers of England! Who in the town is the farmer's equal? What is the position which his brother, his uncle, his cousin holds? He is a shopkeeper, who never has a holiday, and does not know what to do with it when it comes to him; to whom the fresh air of heaven is a stranger; who lives among sugars and oils, and the dust of shoddy, and the size of new clothing. Should such an one take to hunting once a week, even after years of toil, men would point their fingers at him and whisper among themselves that he was as good as ruined. His friends would tell him of his wife and children; and, indeed, would tell him truly, for his customers would fly from him. But nobody grudges the farmer his day's sport! No one thinks that he is cruel to his children and unjust to his wife because he keeps a nag for his amusement, and can find a couple of days in the week to go among his friends. And with what advantages he does this! A farmer will do as much with one horse, will see as much hunting, as an outside member of the hunt will do with four, and, indeed, often more. He is his own head-groom, and has no scruple about bringing his horse out twice a week. He asks no livery-stable keeper what his beast can do, but tries the powers of the animal himself, and keeps in his breast a correct record. When the man from London, having taken all he can out of his first horse, has ridden his second to a stand-still, the farmer trots up on his stout, compact cob, without a sign of distress. He knows that the condition of a hunter and a greyhound should not be the same, and that his horse, to be in good working health, should carry nearly all the hard flesh that he can put upon him. How such an one must laugh in his sleeve at the five hunters of the young swell who, after all, is brought to grief in the middle of the season, because he has got nothing to ride! A farmer's horse is never lame, never unfit to go, never throws out curbs, never breaks down before or behind. Like his master, he is never showy. He does not paw, and prance, and arch his neck, and bid the world admire his beauties; but, like his master, he is useful; and when he is wanted, he can always do his work.

O fortunatus nimium agricola, who has one horse, and that a good one, in the middle of a hunting country!

The Lady Who Rides To Hounds

Among those who hunt there are two classes of hunting people who always like it, and these people are hunting parsons and hunting ladies. That it should be so is natural enough. In the life and habits of parsons and ladies there is much that is antagonistic to hunting, and they who suppress this antagonism do so because they are Nimrods at heart. But the riding of these horsemen under difficulties, horsemen and horsewomen, leaves a strong impression on the casual observer of hunting; for to such an one it seems that the hardest riding is forthcoming exactly where no hard riding should be expected. On the present occasion I will, if you please, confine myself to the lady who rides to hounds, and will begin with an assertion, which will not be contradicted, that the number of such ladies is very much on the increase.

Women who ride, as a rule, ride better than men. They, the women, have always been instructed; whereas men have usually come to ride without any instruction. They are put upon ponies when they are all boys, and put themselves upon their fathers' horses as they become hobbledehoys: and thus they obtain the power of sticking on to the animal while he gallops and jumps, and even while he kicks and shies; and, so progressing, they achieve an amount of horsemanship which answers the purposes of life. But they do not acquire the art of riding with exactness, as women do, and rarely have such hands as a woman has on a horse's mouth. The consequence of this is that women fall less often than men, and the field is not often thrown into the horror which would arise were a lady known to be in a ditch with a horse lying on her.

I own that I like to see three or four ladies out in a field, and I like it the better if I am happy enough to count one or more of them among my own acquaintances. Their presence tends to take off from hunting that character of horseyness, of both fast horseyness and slow horseyness, which has become, not unnaturally, attached to it, and to bring it within the category of gentle sports. There used to prevail an idea that the hunting man was of necessity loud and rough, given to strong drinks, ill adapted for the poetries of life, and perhaps a little prone to make money out of his softer friend. It may now be said that this idea is going out of vogue, and that hunting men are supposed to have that same feeling with regard to their horses, the same and no more, which ladies have for their carriage or soldiers for their swords. Horses are valued simply for the services that they can render, and are only valued highly when they are known to be good servants. That a man may hunt without drinking or swearing, and may possess a nag or two without any propensity to sell it or them for double their value, is now beginning to be understood. The oftener that women are to be seen "out," the more will such improved feelings prevail as to hunting, and the pleasanter will be the field to men who are not horsey, but who may nevertheless be good horsemen.

There are two classes of women who ride to hounds, or, rather, among many possible classifications, there are two to which I will now call attention. There is the lady who rides, and demands assistance; and there is the lady who rides, and demands none. Each always, I may say always, receives all the assistance that she may require; but the difference between the two, to the men who ride with them, is very great. It will, of course, be understood that, as to both these samples of female

Nimrods, I speak of ladies who really ride, not of those who grace the coverts with, and disappear under the auspices of, their papas or their grooms when the work begins.

The lady who rides and demands assistance in truth becomes a nuisance before the run is over, let her beauty be ever so transcendent, her horsemanship ever-so-perfect, and her battery of general feminine artillery ever so powerful. She is like the American woman, who is always wanting your place in a railway carriage, and demanding it, too, without the slightest idea of paying you for it with thanks; whose study it is to treat you as though she ignored your existence while she is appropriating your services. The hunting lady who demands assistance is very particular about her gates, requiring that aid shall be given to her with instant speed, but that the man who gives it shall never allow himself to be hurried as he renders it. And she soon becomes reproachful, oh, so soon! It is marvellous to watch the manner in which a hunting lady will become exacting, troublesome, and at last imperious, deceived and spoilt by the attention which she receives. She teaches herself to think at last that a man is a brute who does not ride as though he were riding as her servant, and that it becomes her to assume indignation if every motion around her is not made with some reference to her safety, to her comfort, or to her success. I have seen women look as Furies look, and heard them speak as Furies are supposed to speak, because men before them could not bury themselves and their horses out of their way at a moment's notice, or because some pulling animal would still assert himself while they were there, and not sink into submission and dog-like obedience for their behoof.

I have now before my eyes one who was pretty, brave, and a good horse-woman; but how men did hate her! When you were in a line with her there was no shaking her off. Indeed, you were like enough to be shaken off yourself, and to be rid of her after that fashion. But while you were with her you never escaped her at a single fence, and always felt that you were held to be trespassing against her in some manner. I shall never forget her voice, "Pray, take care of that gate." And yet it was a pretty voice, and elsewhere she was not given to domineering more than is common to pretty women in general; but she had been taught badly from the beginning, and she was a pest. It was the same at every gap. "Might I ask you not to come too near me?" And yet it was impossible to escape her. Men could not ride wide of her, for she would not ride wide of them. She had always some male escort with her, who did not ride as she rode, and consequently, as she chose to have the advantage of an escort, of various escorts, she was always in the company of some who did not feel as much joy in the presence of a pretty young woman as men should do under all circumstances. "Might I ask you not to come too near me?" If she could only have heard the remarks to which this constant little request of hers gave rise. She is now the mother of children, and her hunting days are gone, and probably she never makes that little request. Doubtless that look, made up partly of offence and partly of female dignity, no longer clouds her brow. But I fancy that they who knew her of old in the hunting field never approach her now without fancying that they hear those reproachful words, and see that powerful look of injured feminine weakness.

But there is the hunting lady who rides hard and never asks for assistance. Perhaps I may be allowed to explain to embryo Dianas, to the growing huntresses of the present age, that she who rides and makes no demand receives attention as close as is ever given to her more imperious sister. And how welcome she is! What a grace she lends to the day's sport! How pleasant it is to see her in her pride of place, achieving her mastery over the difficulties in her way by her own wit, as all men, and all women also, must really do who intend to ride to hounds; and doing it all without any sign that the difficulties are too great for her!

The lady who rides like this is in truth seldom in the way. I have heard men declare that they would never wish to see a side-saddle in the field because women are troublesome, and because they must be treated with attention let the press of the moment be ever so instant. From this I dissent altogether. The small amount of courtesy that is needed is more than atoned for by the grace of her presence, and in fact produces no more impediment in the hunting-field than in other scenes of life. But in the hunting-field, as in other scenes, let assistance never be demanded by a woman. If the lady finds that she cannot keep a place in the first flight without such demands on the patience of those around her, let her acknowledge to herself that the attempt is not in her line, and that it should be abandoned. If it be the ambition of a hunting lady to ride straight, and women have very much of this ambition, let her use her eyes but never her voice; and let her ever have a smile for those who help her in her little difficulties. Let her never ask any one "to take care of that gate," or look as though she expected the profane crowd to keep aloof from her. So shall she win the hearts of those around her, and go safely through brake and brier, over ditch and dyke, and meet with a score of knights around her who will be willing and able to give her eager aid should the chance of any moment require it.

There are two accusations which the more demure portion of the world is apt to advance against hunting ladies, or, as I should better say, against hunting as an amusement for ladies. It leads to flirting, they say, to flirting of a sort which mothers would not approve; and it leads to fast habits, to ways and thoughts which are of the horse horsey, and of the stable, strongly tinged with the rack and manger. The first of these accusations is, I think, simply made in ignorance. As girls are brought up among us now-a-days, they may all flirt, if they have a mind to do so; and opportunities for flirting are much better and much more commodious in the ball-room, in the drawing-room, or in the park, than they are in the hunting-field. Nor is the work in hand of a nature to create flirting tendencies, as, it must be admitted, is the nature of the work in hand when the floors are waxed and the fiddles are going. And this error has sprung from, or forms part of, another, which is wonderfully common among non-hunting folk. It is very widely thought by many, who do not, as a rule, put themselves in opposition to the amusements of the world, that hunting in itself is a wicked thing; that hunting men are fast, given to unclean living and bad ways of life; that they usually go to bed drunk, and that they go about the world roaring hunting cries, and disturbing the peace of the innocent generally. With such men, who could wish that wife, sister, or daughter should associate? But I venture to say that this opinion, which I believe to be common, is erroneous, and that men who hunt are not more iniquitous than men who go out fishing, or play dominoes, or dig in their gardens. Maxima debetur pueris reverentia, and still more to damsels; but if boys and girls will never go where they will hear more to injure them than they will usually do amidst the ordinary conversation of a hunting field, the maxima reverentia will have been attained.

As to that other charge, let it be at once admitted that the young lady who has become of the horse horsey has made a fearful, almost a fatal mistake. And so also has the young man who falls into the same error. I hardly know to which such phase of character may be most injurious. It is a pernicious vice, that of succumbing to the beast that carries you, and making yourself, as it were, his servant, instead of keeping him ever as yours. I will not deny that I have known a lady to fall into this vice from hunting; but so also have I known ladies to marry their music-masters and to fall in love with their footmen. But not on that account are we to have no music-masters and no footmen.

Let the hunting lady, however, avoid any touch of this blemish, remembering that no man ever likes a woman to know as much about a horse as he thinks he knows himself.

The Man Who Hunts And Does Like It

The man who hunts and does like it is an object of keen envy to the man who hunts and doesn't; but he, too, has his own miseries, and I am not prepared to say that they are always less aggravating than those endured by his less ambitious brother in the field. He, too, when he comes to make up his account, when he brings his hunting to book and inquires whether his whistle has been worth its price, is driven to declare that vanity and vexation of spirit have been the prevailing characteristics of his hunting life. On how many evenings has he returned contented with his sport? How many days has he declared to have been utterly wasted? How often have frost and snow, drought and rain, wind and sunshine, impeded his plans? for to a hunting man frost, snow, drought, rain, wind and sunshine, will all come amiss. Then, when the one run of the season comes, he is not there! He has been idle and has taken a liberty with the day; or he has followed other gods and gone with strange hounds. With sore ears and bitter heart he hears the exaggerated boastings of his comrades, and almost swears that he will have no more of it. At the end of the season he tells himself that the season's amusement has cost him five hundred pounds; that he has had one good day, three days that were not bad, and that all the rest have been vanity and vexation of spirit. After all, it may be a question whether the man who hunts and doesn't like it does not have the best of it.

When we consider what is endured by the hunting man the wonder is that any man should like it. In the old days of Squire Western, and in the old days too since the time of Squire Western, the old days of thirty years since, the hunting man had his hunting near to him. He was a country gentleman who considered himself to be energetic if he went out twice a week, and in doing this he rarely left his house earlier for that purpose than he would leave it for others. At certain periods of the year he if ho went out twice a he rarely left his house than he would leave it periods of the year he would, perhaps, be out before dawn; but then the general habits of his life conduced to early rising; and his distances were short. If he kept a couple of horses for the purpose he was well mounted, and these horses were available for other uses. He rode out and home, jogging slowly along the roads, and was a martyr to no ambition. All that has been changed now. The man who hunts and likes it, either takes a small hurting seat away from the comforts of his own home, or he locates himself miserably at an inn, or he undergoes the purgatory of daily journeys up and down from London, doing that for his hunting which no consideration of money-making would induce him to do for his business. His hunting requires from him everything, his time, his money, his social hours, his rest, his sweet morning sleep; nay, his very dinners have to be sacrificed to this Moloch!

Let us follow him on an ordinary day. His groom comes to his bed-chamber at seven o'clock, and tells him that it has frozen during the night. If he be a London man, using the train for his hunting, he knows nothing of the frost, and does not learn whether the day be practicable or not till he finds himself down in the country. But we will suppose our friend to be located in some hunting district, and accordingly his groom visits him with tidings. "Is it freezing now?" he asks from under the bedclothes. And even the man who does like it at such moments almost wishes that the answer should be plainly in the affirmative. Then swiftly again to the arms of Morpheus he might take himself, and ruffle his temper no further on that morning! He desires, at any rate, a decisive answer. To be or not to be as regards that day's hurting is what he now wants to know. But that is exactly what the groom cannot tell him. "It's just a thin crust of frost, sir, and the s'mometer is a standing at the pint." That is the answer which the man makes, and on that he has to come to a decision! For half an hour he lies doubting while his water is getting cold, and then sends for his man again. The thermometer is still standing at the point, but the man has tried the crust with his heel and found it to be very thin. The man who hunts and likes it scorns his ease, and resolves that he will at any rate persevere. He tumbles into his tub, and a little before nine comes out to his breakfast, still doubting sorely whether or no the day "will do." There he, perhaps, meets one or two others like himself, and learns that the men who hunt and don't like it are still warm in their beds. On such mornings as these, and such mornings are very many, the men who hunt and do not like it certainly have the best of it. The man who hunts and does like it takes himself out to some kitchen-garden or neighbouring paddock, and kicks at the ground himself. Certainly there is a crust, a very manifest crust. Though he puts up in the country, he has to go sixteen miles to the meet, and has no means of knowing whether or no the hounds will go out. "Jorrocks always goes if there's a chance," says one fellow, speaking of the master. "I don't know," says our friend; "he's a deal slower at it than he used to be. For my part, I wish Jorrocks would go; he's getting too old." Then he bolts a mutton chop and a couple of eggs hurriedly, and submits himself to be carried off in the trap.

Though he is half an hour late at the meet, no hounds have as yet come, and he begins to curse his luck. A non-hunting day, a day that turns out to be no day for hunting purposes, begun in this way, is of all days the most melancholy. What is a man to do with himself who has put himself into his boots and breeches, and who then finds himself, by one o'clock, landed back at his starting-point without employment? Who under such circumstances can apply himself to any salutary employment? Cigars and stable-talk are all that remain to him; and it is well for him if he can refrain from the additional excitement of brandy and water.

But on the present occasion we will not presume that our friend has fallen into so deep a bathos of misfortune. At twelve o'clock Tom appears, with the hounds following slowly at his heels; and a dozen men, angry with impatience, fly at him with assurances that there has been no sign of frost since ten o'clock. "Ain't there?" says Tom; "you look at the north sides of the banks, and see how you'd like it." Someone makes an uncivil remark as to the north sides of the banks, and wants to know when old Jorrocks is coming. "The squire 'll be here time enough," says Tom. And then there takes place that slow walking up and down of the hounds, which on such mornings always continues for half an hour. Let him who envies the condition of the man who hunts and likes it, remember that a cold thaw is going on, that our friend is already sulky with waiting, that to ride up and down for an hour and a half at a walking pace on such a morning is not an exhilarating pastime, and he will understand that the hunting man himself may have doubts as to the wisdom of his course of action.

But at last Jorrocks is there, and the hounds trot off to cover. So dull has been everything on this morning that even that is something, and men begin to make themselves happier in the warmth of the movement. The hounds go into covert, and a period of excitement is commenced. Our friend who likes hunting remarks to his neighbour that the ground is rideable. His neighbour who doesn't like it quite so well says that he doesn't know. They remain standing close together on a forest ride for twenty minutes, but conversation doesn't go beyond that. The man who doesn't like it has lit a cigar, but the man who does like it never lights a cigar when hounds are drawing.

And now the welcome music is heard, and a fox has been found. Mr. Jorrocks, galloping along the ride with many oaths, implores those around him to hold their tongues and remain quiet. Why he should trouble himself to do this, as he knows that no one will obey his orders, it is difficult to surmise. Or why men should stand still in the middle of a large wood when they expect a fox to break, because Mr. Jorrocks swears at them, is also not to be understood. Our friend pays no attention to Mr. Jorrocks, but makes for the end of the ride, going with ears erect, and listening to the distant hounds as they turn upon the turning fox. As they turn, he returns; and, splashing through the mud of the now softened ground, through narrow tracks, with the boughs in his face, listening always, now hoping, now despairing, speaking to no one, but following and followed, he makes his way backwards and forwards through the wood, till at last, weary with wishing and working, he rests himself in some open spot, and begins to eat his luncheon. It is now past two, and it would puzzle him to say what pleasure he has as yet had out of his day's amusement.

But now, while the flask is yet at his mouth, he hears from some distant corner a sound that tells him that the fox is away. He ought to have persevered, and then he would have been near them. As it is, all that labour of riding has been in vain, and he has before him the double task of finding the line of the hounds and of catching them when he has found it. He has a crowd of men around him; but he knows enough of hunting to be aware that the men who are wrong at such moments are always more numerous than they who are right. He has to choose for himself, and chooses quickly, dashing down a ride to the right, while a host of those who know that he is one of them who like it, follow closely at his heels, too closely, as he finds at the first fence out of the woods, when one of his young admirers almost jumps on the top of him. "Do you want to get into my pocket, sir?" he says, angrily. The young admirer is snubbed, and, turning away, attempts to make a line for himself.

But though he has been followed, he has great doubt as to his own course. To hesitate is to be lost, so he goes on, on rapidly, looking as he clears every fence for the spot at which he is to clear the next; but he is by no means certain of his course. Though he has admirers at his heels who credit him implicitly, his mind is racked by an agony of ignorance. He has got badly away, and the hounds are running well, and it is going to be a good thing; and he will not see it. He has not been in for anything good this year, and now this is his luck! His eye travels round over the horizon as he is gallopping, and though he sees men here and there, he can catch no sign of a hound; nor can he catch the form of any man who would probably be with them. But he perseveres, choosing his points as he goes, till the tail of his followers becomes thinner and thinner. He comes out upon a road, and makes the pace as good as he can along the soft edge of it. He sniffs at the wind, knowing that the fox, going at such a pace as this, must run with it. He tells himself from outward signs where he is, and uses his dead knowledge to direct him. He scorns to ask a question as he passes countrymen in his course, but he would give five guineas to know exactly where the hounds are at that moment. He has been at it now forty minutes, and is in despair. His gallant nag rolls a little under him, and he knows that he has been going too fast. And for what; for what? What good has it all done him? What good will it do him, though he should kill the beast? He curses between his teeth, and everything is vanity and vexation of spirit.

"They've just run into him at Boxall Springs, Mr. Jones," says a farmer whom he passes on the road. Boxall Springs is only a quarter of a mile before him, but he wonders how the farmer has come to know all about it. But on reaching Boxall Springs he finds that the farmer was right, and that Tom is already breaking up the fox. "Very good thing, Mr. Jones," says the squire in good humour. Our friend mutters something between his teeth and rides away in dudgeon from the triumphant master. On his road home he hears all about it from everybody. It seems to him that he alone of all those who are anybody has missed the run, the run of the season! "And killed him in the open as you may say," says Smith, who has already twice boasted in Jones's hearing that he had seen every turn the hounds had made. "It wasn't in the open," says Jones, reduced in his anger to diminish as far as may be the triumph of his rival.

Such is the fate, the too frequent fate of the man who hunts and does like it.

The Man Who Hunts And Doesn't Like It

It seems to be odd, at first sight, that there should be any such men as these; but their name and number is legion. If we were to deduct from the hunting-crowd farmers, and others who hunt because hunting is brought to their door, of the remainder we should find that the "men who don't like it" have the preponderance. It is pretty much the same, I think, with all amusements. How many men go to balls, to races, to the theatre, how many women to concerts and races, simply because it is the thing to do? They have perhaps, a vague idea that they may ultimately find some joy in the pastime; but, though they do the thing constantly, they never like it. Of all such men, the hunting men are perhaps the most to be pitied.

They are easily recognized by anyone who cares to scrutinize the men around him in the hunting field. It is not to be supposed that all those who, in common parlance, do not ride, are to be included among the number of hunting men who don't like it. Many a man who sticks constantly to the roads and lines of gates, who, from principle, never looks at a fence, is much attached to hunting. Some of those who have borne great names as Nimrods in our hunting annals would as life have led a forlorn-hope as put a horse at a flight of hurdles. But they, too, are known; and though the nature of their delight is a mystery to straight-going men, it is manifest enough, that they do like it. Their theory of hunting is at any rate plain. They have an acknowledged system, and know what they are doing. But the men who don't like it, have no system, and never know distinctly what is their own aim. During some portion of their career they commonly try to ride hard, and sometimes for a while they will succeed. In short spurts, while the cherry-brandy prevails, they often have small successes; but even with the assistance of a spur in the head they never like it.

Dear old John Leech! What an eye he had for the man who hunts and doesn't like it! But for such, as a pictorial chronicler of the hunting field he would have had no fame. Briggs, I fancy, in his way did like it. Briggs was a full-blooded, up-apt, awkward, sanguine man, who was able to like anything, from gin and water upwards. But with how many a wretched companion of Briggs' are we not familiar? men as to whom any girl of eighteen would swear from the form of his visage and the carriage of his legs as he sits on his horse that he was seeking honour where honour was not to be found, and looking for pleasure in places where no pleasure lay for him.

But the man who hunts and doesn't like it, has his moments of gratification, and finds a source of pride in his penance. In the summer, hunting does much for him. He does not usually take much personal care of his horses, as he is probably a town man and his horses are summered by a keeper of hunting stables; but he talks of them. He talks of them freely, and the keeper of the hunting stables is occasionally forced to write to him. And he can run down to look at his nags, and spend a few hours eating bad mutton chops, walking about the yards and paddocks, and, bleeding halfcrowns through the nose. In all this there is a delight which offers some compensation for his winter misery to our friend who hunts and doesn't like it.

He finds it pleasant to talk of his horses especially to young women, with whom, perhaps, the ascertained fact of his winter employment does give him some credit. It is still something to be a hunting man even yet, though the multiplicity of railways and the existing plethora of money has so increased the number of sportsmen, that to keep a nag or two near some well-known station, is nearly as common as to die. But the delight of these martyrs is at the highest in the presence of their tailors; or, higher still, perhaps, in that of their bootmakers. The hunting man does receive some honour from him who makes his breeches; and, with a well-balanced sense of justice, the tailor's foreman is, I think, more patient, more admiring, more demonstrative in his assurances, more ready with his bit of chalk, when handling the knee of the man who doesn't like the work, than he ever is with the customer who comes to him simply because he wants some clothes fit for the saddle. The judicious conciliating tradesman knows that compensation should be given, and he helps to give it. But the visits to the bootmaker are better still. The tailor persists in telling his customer how his breeches should be made, and after what fashion they should be worn; but the bootmaker will take his orders meekly. If not ruffled by paltry objections as to the fit of the foot, he will accede to any amount of instructions as to the legs and tops. And then a new pair of top boots is a pretty toy; Costly, perhaps, if needed only as a toy, but very pretty, and more decorative in a gentleman's dressing-room than any other kind of garment. And top boots, when multiplied in such a locality, when seen in a phalanx tell such pleasant lies on their owner's behalf. While your breeches are as dumb in their retirement as though you had not paid for them, your conspicuous boots are eloquent with a thousand tongues! There is pleasure found, no doubt, in this.

As the season draws nigh the delights become vague, and still more vague; but, nevertheless, there are delights. Getting up at six o'clock in November to go down to Bletchley by an early train is not in itself pleasant, but on the opening morning, on the few first opening mornings, there is a promise about the thing which invigorates and encourages the early riser. He means to like it this year if he can. He has still some undefined notion that his period of pleasure will now come. He has not, as yet, accepted the adverse verdict which his own nature has given against him in this matter of hunting, and he gets into his early tub with acme glow of satisfaction. And afterwards it is nice to find himself bright with mahogany tops, buff-tinted breeches, and a pink coat. The ordinary habiliments of an English gentleman are so sombre that his own eye is gratified, and he feels that he has placed himself in the vanguard of society by thus shining in his apparel. And he will ride this year! He is fixed to that purpose. He will ride straight; and, if possible, he will like it.

But the Ethiop cannot change his skin, nor can any man add a cubit to his stature. He doesn't like it, and all around him in the field know how it is with him; he himself knows how it is with others like himself, and he congregates with his brethren. The period of his penance has come upon him. He has to pay the price of those pleasant interviews with his tradesmen. He has to expiate the false boasts made to his female cousins. That row of boots cannot be made to shine in his chamber for nothing. The hounds have found, and the fox is away. Men are fastening on their flat-topped hats and feeling themselves in their stirrups. Horses are hot for the run, and the moment for liking it has come, if only it were possible!

But at moments such as these something has to be done. The man who doesn't like it, let him dislike it ever so much, Cannot check his horse and simply ride back to the hunting stables. He understands that were he to do that, he must throw up his cap at once and resign. Nor can he trot easily along the roads with the fat old country gentleman who is out on his rough cob, and who, looking up to the wind and remembering the position of adjacent coverts, will give a good guess as to the direction in which the field will move. No; he must make an effort. The time of his penance has come, and the penance must be borne. There is a spark of pluck about him, though unfortunately he has brought it to bear in a wrong direction. The blood still runs at his heart, and he resolves that he will ride, if only he could tell which way.

The stout gentleman on the cob has taken the road to the left with a few companions; but our friend knows that the stout gentleman has a little game of his own which will not be suitable for one who intends to ride. Then the crowd in front has divided itself. Those to the right rush down a hill towards a brook with a ford. One or two, men whom he hates with an intensity of envy, have jumped the brook, and have settled to their work. Twenty or thirty others are hustling themselves through the water. The time for a judicious start on that side is already gone. But others, a crowd of others, are facing the big ploughed field immediately before them. That is the straightest riding, and with them he goes. Why has the scent lain so hot over the up-turned heavy ground? Why do they go so fast at this the very first blush of the morning? Fortune is always against him, and the horse is pulling him through the mud as though the brute meant to drag his arm out of the socket. At the first fence, as he is steadying himself, a butcher passes him roughly in the jump and nearly takes away the side of his top boot. He is knocked half out of his saddle, and in that condition scrambles through. When he has regained his equilibrium he sees the happy butcher going into the field beyond. He means to curse the butcher when he catches him, but the butcher is safe. A field and a half before him he still sees the tail hounds, and renews his effort. He has meant to like it to-day, and he will. So he rides at the next fence boldly, where the butcher has left his mark, and does it pretty well, with a slight struggle. Why is it that he can never get over a ditch without some struggle in his saddle, some scramble with his horse? Why does he curse the poor animal so constantly, unless it be that he cannot catch the butcher? Now he rushes at a gate which others have opened for him, but rushes too late and catches his leg. Mad with pain, he nearly gives it up, but the spark of pluck is still there, and with throbbing knee he perseveres. How he hates it! It is all detestable now. He cannot hold his horse because of his gloves, and he cannot get them off. The sympathetic beast knows that his master is unhappy, and makes himself unhappy and troublesome in consequence. Our friend is still going, riding wildly, but still keeping a grain of caution for his fences. He has not been down yet, but has barely saved himself more than once. The ploughs are very deep, and his horse, though still boring at him, pants heavily. Oh, that there might come a check, or that the brute of a fox might happily go to ground! But no! The ruck of the hunt is far away from him in front, and the game is running steadily straight for some well known though still distant protection. But the man who doesn't like it still sees a red coat before him, and perseveres in chasing the wearer of it. The solitary red coat becomes distant, and still more distant from him, but he goes on while he can yet keep the line in which that red coat has ridden. He must hurry himself, however, or he will be lost to humanity, and will be alone. He must hurry himself, but his horse now desires to hurry no more. So he puts his spurs to the brute savagely, and then at some little fence, some ignoble ditch, they come down together in the mud, and the question of any further effort is saved for the rider. When he arises the red coat is out of sight, and his own horse is half across the field before him. In such a position, is it possible that a man should like it?

About four o'clock in the afternoon, when the other men are coming in, he turns up at the hunting stables, and nobody asks him any questions. He may have been doing fairly well for what anybody knows, and, as he says nothing of himself, his disgrace is at any rate hidden. Why should he tell that he had been nearly an hour on foot trying to catch his horse, that he had sat himself down on a bank and almost cried, and that he had drained his flask to the last drop before one o'clock? No one need know the extent of his miseries. And no one does know how great is the misery endured by those who hunt regularly, and who do not like it.

The Master Of Hounds

The master of hounds best known by modern description is the master of the Jorrocks type. Now, as I take it, this is not the type best known by English sportsmen, nor do the Jorrocks ana, good though they be, give any fair picture of such a master of hounds as ordinarily presides over the hunt in English counties. Mr. Jorrocks comes into a hunt when no one else can be found to undertake the work; when, in want of any one better, the subscribers hire his services as those of an upper servant; when, in fact, the hunt is at a low ebb, and is struggling for existence. Mr. Jorrocks with his carpet-bag then makes his appearance, driving the hardest bargain that he can, purposing to do the country at the lowest possible figure, followed by a short train of most undesirable nags, with reference to which the wonder is that Mr. Jorrocks should be able to induce any hunting servant to trust his neck to their custody. Mr. Jorrocks knows his work, and is generally a most laborious man. Hunting is his profession, but it is one by which he can barely exist. He hopes to sell a horse or two during the season, and in this way adds something of the trade of a dealer to his other trade. But his office is thankless, ill-paid, closely watched, and subject to all manner of indignities. Men suspect him, and the best of those who ride with him will hardly treat him as their equal. He is accepted as a disagreeable necessity, and is dismissed as soon as the country can do better for itself. Any hunt that has subjected itself to Mr. Jorrocks knows that it is in disgrace, and will pass its itinerant master on to some other district as soon as it can suit itself with a proper master of the good old English sort.

It is of such a master as this, a master of the good old English sort, and not of an itinerant contractor for hunting, that I here intend to speak. Such a master is usually an old resident in the county which he hunts; one of those country noblemen or gentlemen whose parks are the glory of our English landscape, and whose names are to be found in the pages of our county records; or if not that, he is one who, with a view to hunting, has brought his family and fortune into a new district, and has found a ready place as a country gentleman among new neighbours. It has been said that no one should become a member of Parliament unless he be a man of fortune. I hold such a rule to be much more true with reference to a master of hounds. For his own sake this should be so, and much more so for the sake of those over whom he has to preside. It is a position in which no man can be popular without wealth, and it is a position which no man should seek to fill unless he be prepared to spend his money for the gratification of others. It has been said of masters of hounds that they must always have their hands in their pockets, and must always have a guinea to find there; and nothing can be truer than this if successful hunting is to be expected. Men have hunted countries, doubtless, on economical principles, and the sport has been carried on from year to year; but under such circumstances it is ever dwindling and becoming frightfully less. The foxes disappear, and when found almost instantly sink below ground. Distant coverts, which are ever the best because less frequently drawn, are deserted, for distance of course adds greatly to expense. The farmers round the centre of the county become sullen, and those beyond are indifferent; and so, from bad to worse, the famine goes on till the hunt has perished of atrophy. Grease to the wheels, plentiful grease to the wheels, is needed in all machinery; but I know of no machinery in which everrunning grease is so necessary as in the machinery of hunting.

Of such masters as I am now describing there are two sorts, of which, however, the one is going rapidly and, I think, happily out of fashion. There is the master of hounds who takes a subscription, and the master who takes none. Of the latter class of sportsman, of the imperial head of a country who looks upon the coverts of all his neighbours as being almost his own property, there are, I believe, but few left. Nor is such imperialism fitted for the present age. In the days of old of which we read so often, the days of Squire Western, when fox-hunting was still young among us, this was the fashion in which all hunts were maintained. Any country gentleman who liked the sport kept a small pack of hounds, and rode over his own lands or the lands of such of his neighbours as had no similar establishments of their own. We never hear of Squire Western that he hunted the county, or that he went far afield to his meets. His tenants joined him, and by degrees men came to his hunt from greater distances around him. As the necessity for space increased, increasing from increase of hunting ambition, the richer and more ambitious squires began to undertake the management of wider areas, and so our hunting districts were formed. But with such extension of area there came, of course, necessity of extended expenditure, and so the fashion of subscription lists arose. There have remained some few great Nimrods who have chosen to be magnanimous and to pay for everything, despising the contributions of their followers. Such a one was the late Earl Fitzhardinge, and after such manner in, as I believe, the Berkeley hunt still conducted. But it need hardly be explained, that as hunting is now conducted in England, such a system is neither fair nor palatable. It is not fair that so great a cost for the amusement of other men should fall upon any one man's pocket; nor is it palatable to others that such unlimited power should be placed in any one man's hands. The ordinary master of subscription hounds is no doubt autocratic, but he is not autocratic with all the power of tyranny which belongs to the despot who rules without taxation. I doubt whether any master of a subscription pack would advertise his meets for eleven, with an understanding that the hounds were never to move till twelve, when he intended to be present in person. Such was the case with Lord Fitzhardinge, and I do not know that it was generally thought that he carried his power too far. And I think, too, that gentlemen feel that they ride with more pleasure when they themselves contribute to the cost of their own amusement.

Our master of hounds shall be a country gentleman who takes a subscription, and who therefore, on becoming autocratic, makes himself answerable to certain general rules for the management of his autocracy. He shall hunt not less, let us say, than three days a week; but though not less, it will be expected probably that he will hunt oftener. That is, he will advertise three days and throw a byeday in for the benefit of his own immediate neighbourhood; and these byedays, it must be known, are the cream of hunting, for there is no crowd, and the foxes break sooner and run straighter. And he will be punctual to his time, giving quarter to none and asking none himself. He will draw fairly through the day, and indulge no caprices as to coverts. The laws, indeed, are never written, but they exist and are understood; and when they be too recklessly disobeyed, the master of hounds falls from his high place and retires into private life, generally with a broken heart. In the hunting field, as in all other communities, republics, and governments, the power of the purse is everything. As long as that be retained, the despotism of the master is tempered and his rule will be beneficent.

Five hundred pounds a day is about the sum which a master should demand for hunting an average country, that is, so many times five hundred pounds a year as he may hunt days in the week. If four days a week be required of him, two thousand a year will be little enough. But as a rule, I think masters are generally supposed to charge only for the advertised days, and to give the byedays out of their own pocket. Nor must it be thought that the money so subscribed will leave the master free of expense. As I have said before, he should be a rich man. Whatever be the subscription paid to him, he must go beyond it, very much beyond it, or there will grow up against him a feeling that he is mean, and that feeling will rob him of all his comfort. Hunting men in England wish to pay for their own amusement; but they desire that more shall be spent than they pay. And in this there is a rough justice, that roughness of justice which pervades our English institutions. To a master of hounds is given a place of great influence, and into his hands is confided an authority the possession of which among his fellow-sportsmen is very pleasant to him. For this he is expected to pay, and he does pay for it. A Lord Mayor is, I take it, much in the same category. He has a salary as Lord Mayor, but if he do not spend more than that on his office he becomes a byword for stinginess among Lord Mayors To be Lord Mayor is his whistle, and he pays for it.

For myself, if I found myself called upon to pay for one whistle or the other, I would sooner be a master of hounds than a Lord Mayor. The power is certainly more perfect, and the situation, I think, more splendid. The master of hounds has no aldermen, no common council, no liverymen. As long as he fairly performs his part of the compact, he is altogether without control. He is not unlike the captain of a man-of-war; but, unlike the captain of a man-of-war, he carries no sailing orders. He is free to go where he lists, and is hardly expected to tell any one whither he goeth. He is enveloped in a mystery which, to the young, adds greatly to his grandeur; and he is one of those who, in spite of the democratic tenderness of the age, may still be said to go about as a king among men. No one contradicts him. No one speaks evil of him to his face; and men tremble when they have whispered anything of some half-drawn covert, of some unstopped earth, some fox that should not have escaped, and, looking round, see that the master is within earshot. He is flattered, too, if that be of any avail to him. How he is flattered! What may be done in this way to Lord Mayors by common councilmen who like Mansion-house crumbs, I do not know; but kennel crumbs must be very sweet to a large class of sportsmen. Indeed, they are so sweet that almost every man will condescend to flatter the master of hounds. And ladies too, all the pretty girls delight to be spoken to by the master! He needs no introduction, but is free to sip all the sweets that come. Who will not kiss the toe of his boots, or refuse to be blessed by the sunshine of his smile?

But there are heavy duties, deep responsibilities, and much true heart-felt anxiety to stand as makeweight against all these sweets. The master of hounds, even though he take no part in the actual work of hunting his own pack, has always his hands full of work. He is always learning, and always called upon to act on his knowledge suddenly. A Lord Mayor may sit at the Mansionhouse, I think, without knowing much of the law. He may do so without discovery of his ignorance. But the master of hounds who does not know his business is seen through at once. To say what that business is would take a paper longer than this, and the precept writer by no means considers himself equal to such a task. But it is multifarious, and demands a special intellect for itself. The master should have an eye like an eagle's, an ear like a thief's, and a heart like a dog's that can be either soft or ruthless as occasion may require. How he should love his foxes, and with what pertinacity he should kill them! How he should rejoice when his skill has assisted in giving the choice men of his hunt a run that they can remember for the next six years! And how heavy should be his heart within him when he trudges home with them, weary after a blank day, to the misery of which his incompetency has, perhaps, contributed! A master of hounds should be an anxious man; so anxious that the privilege of talking to pretty girls should be of little service to him.

One word I will say as to the manners of a master of hounds, and then I will have done. He should be an urbane man, but not too urbane; and he should certainly be capable of great austerity. It used to be said that no captain of a man-of-war could hold his own without swearing. I will not quite say the same of a master of hounds, or the old ladies who think hunting to be wicked will have a handle against me. But I will declare that if any man could be justified in swearing, it would be a master of hounds. The troubles of the captain are as nothing to his. The captain has the ultimate power of the sword, or at any rate of the fetter, in his hands, while the master has but his own tongue to trust, his tongue and a certain influence which his position gives him. The master who can make that influence suffice without swearing is indeed a great man. Now-a-days swearing is so distasteful to the world at large, that great efforts are made to rule without it, and some such efforts are successful; but any man who has hunted for the last twenty years will bear me out in saying that hard words in a master's mouth used to be considered indispensable. Now and then a little irony is tried. "I wonder, sir, how much you'd take to go home?" I once heard a master ask of a red-coated stranger who was certainly more often among the hounds than he need have been. "Nothing on earth, sir, while you carry on as you are doing just at present," said the stranger. The master accepted the compliment, and the stranger sinned no more.

There are some positions among mankind which are so peculiarly blessed that the owners of them seem to have been specially selected by Providence for happiness on earth in a degree sufficient to raise the malice and envy of all the world around. An English country gentleman with ten thousand a year must have been so selected. Members of Parliament with seats for counties have been exalted after the same unjust fashion. Popular masters of old-established hunts sin against their fellows in the same way. But when it comes to a man to fill up all these positions in England, envy and malice must be dead in the land if he be left alive to enjoy their fruition.

The Hunting Parson

I feel some difficulty in dealing with the character I am now about to describe. The world at large is very prone to condemn the hunting parson, regarding him as a man who is false to his profession; and, for myself, I am not prepared to say that the world is wrong. Had my pastors and masters, my father and mother, together with the other outward circumstances of my early life, made a clergyman of me, I think that I should not have hunted, or at least, I hope that I might have abstained; and yet, for the life of me, I cannot see the reason against it, or tell any man why a clergyman should not ride to hounds. In discussing the subject, and I often do discuss it, the argument against the practice which is finally adopted, the argument which is intended to be conclusive, simply amounts to this, that a parish clergyman who does his duty cannot find the time. But that argument might be used with much more truth against other men of business, against those to whose hunting the world takes no exception. Indeed, of all men, the ordinary parish clergyman, is, perhaps, the least liable to such censure. He lives in the country, and can hunt cheaper and with less sacrifice of time than other men. His professional occupation does not absorb all his hours, and he is too often an idle man, whether he hunt or whether he do not. Nor is it desirable that any man should work always and never play. I think it is certainly the fact that a clergyman may hunt twice a week with less objection in regard to his time than any other man who has to earn his bread by his profession. Indeed, this is so manifestly the case, that I am sure that the argument in question, though it is the one which is always intended to be conclusive, does not in the least convey the objection which is really felt. The truth is, that a large and most respectable section of the world still regards hunting as wicked. It is supposed to be like the Cider Cellars or the Haymarket at twelve o'clock at night. The old ladies know that the young men go to these wicked places, and hope that no great harm is done; but it would be dreadful to think that clergymen should so degrade themselves. Now I wish I could make the old ladies understand that hunting is not wicked.

But although that expressed plea as to the want of time really amounts to nothing, and although the unexpressed feeling of old ladies as to the wickedness of hunting does not in truth amount to much, I will not say that there is no other impediment in the way of a hunting parson. Indeed, there have come up of late years so many impediments in the way of any amusement on the part of clergymen, that we must almost presume them to be divested at their consecration of all human attributes except hunger and thirst. In my younger days, and I am not as yet very old, an elderly clergyman might play his rubber of whist whilst his younger reverend brother was dancing a quadrille; and they might do this without any risk of a rebuke from a bishop, or any probability that their neighbours would look askance at them. Such recreations are now unclerical in the highest degree, or if not in the highest, they are only one degree less so than hunting. The theatre was especially a respectable clerical resource, and we may still occasionally see heads of colleges in the stalls, or perhaps a dean, or some rector, unambitious of further promotion. But should a young curate show himself in the pit, he would be but a lost sheep of the house of Israel. And latterly there went forth, at any rate in one diocese, a firman against cricket! Novels, too, are forbidden; though the fact that they may be enjoyed in solitude saves the clergy from absolute ignorance as to that branch of our national literature. All this is hard upon men who, let them struggle as they may to love the asceticisms of a religious life, are only men; and it has a strong tendency to keep out of the Church that very class, the younger sons of country gentlemen, whom all Churchmen should wish to see enter it. Young men who think of the matter when the time for taking orders is coming near, do not feel themselves qualified to rival St. Paul in their lives; and they who have not thought of it find themselves to be cruelly used when they are expected to make the attempt.

But of all the amusements which a layman may follow and a clergyman may not, hunting is thought to be by much the worst. There is a savour of wickedness about it in the eyes of the old ladies which almost takes it out of their list of innocent amusements even for laymen. By the term old ladies it will be understood, perhaps, that I do not allude simply to matrons and spinsters who may be over the age of sixty, but to that most respectable portion of the world which has taught itself to abhor the pomps and vanities. Pomps and vanities are undoubtedly bad, and should be abhorred; but it behooves those who thus take upon themselves the duties of censors to be sure that the practices abhorred are in truth real pomps and actual vanities, not pomps and vanities of the imagination. Now as to hunting, I maintain that it is of itself the most innocent amusement going, and that it has none of that Cider-Cellar flavour with which the old ladies think that it is so savoury. Hunting is done by a crowd; but men who meet together to do wicked things meet in small parties. Men cannot gamble in the hunting-field, and drinking there is more difficult than in almost any other scene of life. Anonyma, as we were told the other day, may show herself; but if so, she rides alone. The young man must be a brazen sinner, too far gone for hunting to hurt him, who will ride with Anonyma in the field. I know no vice which hunting either produces or renders probable, except the vice of extravagance; and to that, if a man be that way given, every pursuit in life will equally lead him A seat for a Metropolitan borough, or a love of ortolans, or a taste even for new boots will ruin a man who puts himself in the way of ruin. The same may be said of hunting, the same and no more.

But not the less is the general feeling very strong against the hunting parson; and not the less will it remain so in spite of anything that I may say. Under these circumstances our friend the hunting parson usually rides as though he were more or less under a cloud. The cloud is not to be seen in a melancholy brow or a shamed demeanour; for the hunting parson will have lived down those feelings, and is generally too forcible a man to allow himself to be subjected to such annoyances; nor is the cloud to be found in any gentle tardiness of his motions, or an attempt at suppressed riding; for the hunting parson generally rides hard. Unless he loved hunting much he would not be there. But the cloud is to be perceived and heard in the manner in which he speaks of himself and his own doings. He is never natural in his self-talk as is any other man. He either flies at his own cloth at once, marring some false apology for his presence, telling you that he is there just to see the hounds, and hinting to you his own know ledge that he has no business to ride after them; or else he drops his profession altogether, and speaks to you in a tone which makes you feel that you would not dare to speak to him about his parish. You can talk to the banker about his banking, the brewer about his brewing, the farmer about his barley, or the landlord about his land; but to a hunting parson of this latter class, you may not say a word about his church.

There are three modes in which a hunting parson may dress himself for hunting, the variations having reference solely to the nether man. As regards the upper man there can never be a difference. A chimney-pot hat, a white neckerchief, somewhat broad in its folds and strong with plentiful starch, a stout black coat, cut rather shorter than is common with clergymen, and a modest, darksome waistcoat that shall attract no attention, these are all matters of course. But the observer, if he will allow his eye to descend below these upper garments, will perceive that the clergyman may be comfortable and bold in breeches, or he may be uncomfortable and semi-decorous in black trowsers. And there is another mode of dress open to him, which I can assure my readers is not an unknown costume, a tertium quid, by which semi-decorum and comfort are combined. The hunting breeches are put on first, and the black trowsers are drawn over them.

But in whatever garb the hunting parson may ride, he almost invariably rides well, and always enjoys the sport. If he did not, what would tempt him to run counter, as he does, to his bishop and the old ladies? And though, when the hounds are first dashing out of covert, and when the sputtering is beginning and the eager impetuosity of the young is driving men three at a time into the same gap, when that wild excitement of a fox just away is at its height, and ordinary sportsmen are rushing for places, though at these moments the hunting parson may be able to restrain himself, and to declare by his momentary tranquillity that he is only there to see the hounds, he will ever be found, seeing the hounds also, when many of that eager crowd have lagged behind, altogether out of sight of the last tail of them. He will drop into the running, as it were out of the clouds, when the select few have settled down steadily to their steady work; and the select few will never look upon him as one who, after that, is likely to fall out of their number. He goes on certainly to the kill, and then retires a little out of the circle, as though he had trotted in at that spot from his ordinary parochial occupations, just to see the hounds.

For myself I own that I like the hunting parson. I generally find him to be about the pleasantest man in the field, with the most to say for himself, whether the talk be of hunting, of politics, of literature, or of the country. He is never a hunting man unalloyed, unadulterated, and unmixed, a class of man which is perhaps of all classes the most tedious and heavy in hand. The tallow-chandler who can talk only of candles, or the barrister who can talk only of his briefs, is very bad; but the hunting man who can talk only of his runs, is, I think, worse even than the unadulterated tallow-chandler, or the barrister unmixed. Let me pause for a moment here to beg young sportsmen not to fall into this terrible mistake. Such bores in the field are, alas, too common; but the hunting parson never sins after that fashion. Though a keen sportsman, he is something else besides a sportsman, and for that reason, if for no other, is always a welcome addition to the crowd.

But still I must confess at the end of this paper, as I hinted also at the beginning of it, that the hunting parson seems to have made a mistake. He is kicking against the pricks, and running counter to that section of the world which should be his section. He is making himself to stink in the nostrils of his bishop, and is becoming a stumbling-block, and a rock of offence to his brethren. It is bootless for him to argue, as I have here argued, that his amusement is in itself innocent, and that some open-air recreation is necessary to him. Grant him that the bishops and old ladies are wrong and that he is right in principle, and still he will not be justified. Whatever may be our walk in life, no man can walk well who does not walk with the esteem of his fellows. Now those little walks by the covert sides, those pleasant little walks of which I am writing, are not, unfortunately, held to be estimable, or good for themselves, by English clergymen in general.

The Man Who Hunts And Never Jumps

The British public who do not hunt believe too much in the jumping of those who do. It is thought by many among the laity that the hunting man is always in the air, making clear flights over five-barred gates, six-foot walls, and double posts and rails, at none of which would the average hunting man any more think of riding than he would at a small house. We used to hear much of the Galway Blazers, and it was supposed that in County Galway a stiff-built wall six feet high was the sort of thing that you customarily met from field to field when hunting in that comfortable county. Such little impediments were the ordinary food of a real Blazer, who was supposed to add another foot of stonework and a sod of turf when desirous of making himself conspicuous in his moments of splendid ambition. Twenty years ago I rode in Galway now and then, and I found the six-foot walls all shorn of their glory, and that men whose necks were of any value were very anxious to have some preliminary knowledge of the nature of the fabric, whether for instance it might be solid or built of loose stones, before they trusted themselves to an encounter with a wall of four feet and a half. And here, in England, history, that nursing mother of fiction, has given hunting men honours which they here never fairly earned. The traditional five-barred gate is, as a rule, used by hunting men as it was intended to be used by the world at large; that is to say, they open it; and the double posts and rails which look so very pretty in the sporting pictures, are thought to be very ugly things whenever an idea of riding at them presents itself. It is well that mothers should know, mothers full of fear for their boys who are beginning, that the necessary jumping of the hunting field is not after all of so very tremendous a nature; and it may be well also to explain to them and to others that many men hunt with great satisfaction to themselves who never by any chance commit themselves to the peril of a jump, either big or little.

And there is much excellent good sense in the mode of riding adopted by such gentlemen. Some men ride for hunting, some for jumping, and some for exercise; some, no doubt, for all three of these things. Given a man with a desire for the latter, no taste for the second, and some partiality for the first, and he cannot do better than ride in the manner I am describing. He may be sure that he will not find himself alone; and he may be sure also that he will incur none of that ridicule which the non-hunting man is disposed to think must be attached to such a pursuit. But the man who hunts and never jumps, who deliberately makes up his mind that he will amuse himself after that fashion, must always remember his resolve, and be true to the conduct which he has laid down for himself. He must jump not at all. He must not jump a little, when some spurt or spirit may move him, or he will infallibly find himself in trouble. There was an old Duke of Beaufort who was a keen and practical sportsman, a master of hounds, and a known Nimrod on the face of the earth; but he was a man who hunted and never jumped. His experience was perfect, and he was always true to his resolution. Nothing ever tempted him to cross the smallest fence. He used to say of a neighbour of his, who was not so constant, "Jones is an ass. Look at him now. There he is, and he can't get out. Jones doesn't like jumping, but he jumps a little, and I see him pounded every day. I never jump at all, and I'm always free to go where I like." The Duke was certainly right, and Jones was certainly wrong. To get into a field, and then to have no way of getting out of it, is very uncomfortable. As long as you are on the road you have a way open before you to every spot on the world's surface, open, or capable of being opened; or even if incapable of being opened, not positively detrimental to you as long as you are on the right side. But that feeling of a prison under the open air is very terrible, and is rendered almost agonizing by the prisoner's consciousness that his position is the result of his own imprudent temerity, of an audacity which falls short of any efficacious purpose. When hounds are running, the hunting man should always, at any rate, be able to ride on, to ride in some direction, even though it be in a wrong direction. He can then flatter himself that he is riding wide and making a line for himself. But to be entrapped into a field without any power of getting out of it; to see the red backs of the forward men becoming smaller and smaller in the distance, till the last speck disappears over some hedge; to see the fence before you and know that it is too much for you; to ride round and round in an agony of despair which is by no means mute, and at last to give sixpence to some boy to conduct you back into the road; that is wretched: that is real unhappiness. I am, therefore, very persistent in my advice to the man who purposes to hunt without jumping. Let him not jump at all. To jump, but only to jump a little, is fatal. Let him think of Jones.

The man who hunts and doesn't jump, presuming him not to be a duke or any man greatly established as a Nimrod in the hunting world, generally comes out in a black coat and a hat, so that he may not be specially conspicuous in his deviations from the line of the running. He began his hunting probably in search of exercise, but has gradually come to add a peculiar amusement to that pursuit; and of a certain phase of hunting he at last learns more than most of those who ride closest to the hounds. He becomes wonderfully skillful in surmising the line which a fox may probably take, and in keeping himself upon roads parallel to the ruck of the horsemen. He is studious of the wind, and knows to a point of the compass whence it is blowing. He is intimately conversant with every covert in the country; and, beyond this, is acquainted with every earth in which foxes have had their nurseries, or are likely to locate them. He remembers the drains on the different farms in which the hunted animal may possible take refuge, and has a memory even for rabbit-holes. His eye becomes accustomed to distinguish the form of a moving horseman over half-a-dozen fields; and let him see but a cap of any leading man, and he will know which way to turn himself. His knowledge of the country is correct to a marvel. While the man who rides straight is altogether ignorant of his whereabouts, and will not even distinguish the woods through which he has ridden scores of times, the man who rides and never jumps always knows where he is with the utmost accuracy. Where parish is divided from parish and farm from farm, has been a study to him; and he has learned the purpose and bearing of every lane. He is never thrown out, and knows the nearest way from every point to point. If there be a line of gates across from one road to another he will use them, but he will commit himself to a line of gates on the land of no farmer who uses padlocks.

As he trots along the road, occasionally breaking into a gallop when he perceives from some sign known to him that the hunt is turning from him, he is generally accompanied by two or three unfortunates who have lost their way and have straggled from the hounds; and to them he is a guide, philosopher, and friend. He is good-natured for the moment, and patronizes the lost ones. He informs them that they are at last in the right way, and consoles them by assurances that they have lost nothing.

"The fox broke, you know, from the sharp corner of Granby-wood," he says; "the only spot that the crowd had left for him. I saw him come out, standing on the bridge in the road. Then he ran up-wind as far as Green's barn." "Of course he did," says one of the unfortunates who thinks he remembers something of a barn in the early part of the performance. "I was with the three or four first as far as that." "There were twenty men before the hounds there," says our man of the road, who is not without a grain of sarcasm, and can use it when he is strong on his own ground. "Well, he turned there, and ran back very near the corner; but he was headed by a sheep-dog, luckily, and went to the left across the brook." "Ah, that's where I lost them," says one unfortunate. "I was with them miles beyond that," says another. "There were five or six men rode the brook," continues our philosopher, who names the four or five, not mentioning the unfortunate who had spoken last as having been among the number. "Well; then he went across by Ashby Grange, and tried the drain at the back of the farmyard, but Bootle had had it stopped. A fox got in there one day last March, and Bootle always stops it since that. So he had to go on, and he crossed the turnpike close by Ashby Church. I saw him cross, and the hounds were then full five minutes behind him. He went through Frolic Wood, but he didn't hang a minute, and right up the pastures to Morley Hall." "That's where I was thrown out," says the unfortunate who had boasted before, and who is still disposed to boast a little. But our philosopher assures him that he has not in truth been near Morley Hall; and when the unfortunate one makes an attempt to argue, puts him down thoroughly. "All I can say is, you couldn't have been there and be here too at this moment. Morley Hall is a mile and a half to our right, and now they're coming round to the Linney. He'll go into the little wood there, and as there isn't as much as a nutshell open for him, they'll kill him there. It'll have been a tidy little thing, but not very fast. I've hardly been out of a trot yet, but we may as well move on now." Then he breaks into an easy canter by the side of the road, while the unfortunates, who have been rolling among the heavy-ploughed ground in the early part of the day, make vain efforts to ride by his side. They keep him, however, in sight, and are comforted; for he is a man with a character, and knows what he is about. He will never be utterly lost, and as long as they can remain in his company they will not be subjected to that dreadful feeling of absolute failure which comes upon an inexperienced sportsman when he finds himself quite alone, and does not know which way to turn himself.

A man will not learn to ride after this fashion in a day, nor yet in a year. Of all fashions of hunting it requires, perhaps, the most patience, the keenest observation, the strongest memory, and the greatest efforts of intellect. But the power, when achieved, has its triumph; it has its respect, and it has its admirers. Our friend, while he was guiding the unfortunates on the road, knew his position, and rode for a while as though he were a chief of men. He was the chief of men there. He was doing what he knew how to do, and was not failing. He had made no boasts which stern facts would afterwards disprove. And when he rode up slowly to the wood-side, having from a distance heard the huntsman's whoop that told him of the fox's fate, he found that he had been right in every particular. No one at that moment knows the line they have all ridden as well as he knows it. But now, among the crowd, when men are turning their horses' heads to the wind, and loud questions are being asked, and false answers are being given, and the ambitious men are congratulating themselves on their deeds, he sits by listening in sardonic silence. "Twelve miles of ground !" he says to himself, repeating the words of some valiant youngster; "if it's eight, I'll eat it." And then when he hears, for he is all ear as well as all eye, when he hears a slight boast from one of his late unfortunate companions, a first small blast of the trumpet which will become loud anon if it be not checked, he smiles inwardly, and moralizes on the weakness of human nature. But the man who never jumps is not usually of a benevolent nature, and it is almost certain that he will make up a little story against the boaster.

Such is the amusement of the man who rides and never jumps. Attached to every hunt there will be always one or two such men. Their evidence is generally reliable; their knowledge of the country is not to be doubted; they seldom come to any severe trouble; and have usually made for themselves a very wide circle of hunting acquaintances by whom they are quietly respected. But I think that men regard them as they do the chaplain on board a man-of-war, or as they would regard a herald on a field of battle. When men are assembled for fighting, the man who notoriously does not fight must feel himself to be somewhat lower than his brethren around him, and must be so esteemed by others.

Anthony Trollope was one the major English novelists and writers of the Victorian Age. He was also among the most prolific ones, having published forty-seven novels in addition to a number of short stories, Sketches, travelogues and biographies. Trollope succeeded in earning a good reputation as a serious writer during his lifetime and although this reputation seemed to wane during his twilight years and right after his death, the recognition of his genius and literary merits was posthumously revived by critics and academics towards the mid-twentieth century. In addition to being such a successful writer, Trollope had also made a long career as a post office clerk and is today remembered as the inventor of the Victorian post pillar box used to deposit mail before it is collected and forwarded to addressees by the Royal Mail.

Childhood Years

Anthony Trollope was born in London on April 24th, 1815. His family, which emerged from the landed gentry, had yet to go through serious financial problems. This caused little Anthony to suffer the predicament of being educated among the wealthy in the most prestigious London schools while being in rags and impecunious. Although Trollope's father was an educated man and a barrister, he was a complete failure in courts and even his attempts at farming were vain. This pushed Trollope's mother, Frances Trollope, to travel to travel to America in 1827 in search for a more decent income for the family. For financial reasons, Anthony Trollope had to move from one school to another. In the beginning, he attended Harrow School as a day-boy to leave it for a private school in Sunbury and later for another in Winchester. At the age of 15, he returned to Harrow, but he never succeeded in making it to university.

In 1834, Anthony's father, Thomas Trollope, was forced to leave his home country and seek exile in Belgium for unpaid debts. The father, who took his family with him and settled in Bruges, died the following year. After his death, there was finally some financial improvement when Frances Trollope's first publication entitled *Domestic manners of the Americans* (1832) started to achieve considerable success among English readers.

Adulthood and Early works

By that time, Anthony Trollope worked as an usher in a Belgian school before becoming a post office clerk in London. Trollope spent almost seven years in that position without coming to any palpable achievements. It was only in 1841 that a turning point in his life took place when, on his own demand, he was transferred to another postal position in Ireland. He settled in Banagher and was assigned the mission of inspecting post offices all over the country. In addition to the financial advantages that the new position offered, it also enabled him to socialize with the Irish and to have much time to concentrate on writing, mainly on the many train trips to the different offices that he had to visit.

In Ireland, Trollope seemed to transform into another man. He got rid of his childhood shyness and awkwardness and made acquaintances that would later help him populate his novels. Unexpectedly, the English writer had a very positive impression about the Irish whom he found much more good-humored, humane and intelligent that the English. Trollope's ideas about Ireland and Irish people were depicted in a number of his novels such as *The Macdermots of Ballycloran* (1847) and *The Kellys and the O'Kellys* (1848). These early novels did not achieve any significant success, however. According to critics, no English author of the time could arouse any interest among his countrymen by writing about the Irish.

In the early 1840s, Trollope met the daughter of an English banker named Rose Heseltine in the seaside town of Kingstown. They fell in love and got married in 1844. After settling in the south of Ireland where Trollope occupied a new postal position, the couple had two sons. During this period, Trollope travelled a lot and his job offered him the opportunity to visit numerous countries including Scotland, the West Indies and Egypt. It was also during this period that Trollope devoted most of his time and energy to writing and publishing.

Major Achievements

Before returning to London in 1859, Trollope had already started publishing his Barsetshire series of novels. The first novel of the series was *The Warden* which was published in 1855 and represented Trollope's earliest success. The next five novels that Trollope published shared with *The Warden* the same imaginary setting of the county of Barsetshire. They are respectively: *Barchester Towers, Doctor Thorne, Framley Parsonage, The Small House at Allington*, and *The Last Chronicle of Barset*. By the time of the publication of his last Barsetshire novel in 1867, Trollope decided to resign from the Post Office. Having made quite a respectable income from his writing activities, he wanted to spare more time for his publishing and editorial activities. The resignation from his civil position would also allow him to apply for a seat in the House of Commons, something that he had always dreamt of. His dream did not come true, nonetheless, since he was ranked last in the elections after running for the position and spending a considerable amount of money on the campaign.

The success of the Barsetshire novels was a rising crescendo as every new publication sold much more than the one preceding it. The novels were mostly comic examinations of the different facets of Victorian life with much sarcasm and satire. Generally, Trollope's narratives offered a thorough analysis of the main political issues and social structures of the Victorian Age. They combined criticism with smooth humor. Many of Trollope's heroes reappear in more than one work and some characters, such as Mr. Crawley, Mr. Slope and Mrs. Proudie, soon became popular icons in the minds of English readers. By that time, Trollope was introduced to London literary circles and befriended some major figures such as William Makepeace Thackeray, George Eliot, George Murray Smith and G. H. Lewes.

Meanwhile, *Orley Farm* was serially published between 1861 and 1862, and in 1864, Trollope started a new series of novels, the Palliser series. The first of these novels was entitled *Can You Forgive Her?* This was followed by *Phineas Finn* (1869), *The Eustace Diamonds* (1873), *Phineas Redux* (1876), *The Prime Minister (*1876) and *The Duke's Children* (1880). As their title suggests, such novels dealt with the Victorian political issues of the day besides their interest in family relations and the Victorian institution of marriage.

However, apart from the Palliser series, Trollope also published a number of novels which were also quite successful. They include *He Knew He Was Right* which was published in the form of a series between 1868 and 1869 and follows the martial life of a jealous husband and a stubborn wife. In 1871, Trollope wrote another novel entitled, *Lady Anna*, while being on his trip to visit one of his sons in Australia. Soon after his return to England, he published *Australia and New Zealand*. The latter was a travelogue in which he described his experiences and impressions after the visit.

However, it was in 1875 that Trollope published what many readers and critics believe to be his masterpiece, *The Way We Live Now*. The book is a satirical novel which takes a very harsh stance on Victorian society. It mainly denounces its excessive materialism and moral decadence.

Twilight

Anthony Trollope's biographers agree that the novelist's literary reputation sank during his last years and the few decades after his death to be revived only in the middle of the twentieth century. This was caused by different factors. First, there was the scathing criticism that he directed towards his countrymen and Australians, among others. Second, many English critics and literary men did not appreciate Trollope's profuse literary production and thought that this could only be explained by his mechanical style of writing. The latter idea was further strengthened after the posthumous publication of Trollope's autobiography in which he revealed that he used to set schedules and deadlines for his writings. For literary purists, this was against the principle of literary spontaneity and inspiration. Furthermore, the reaction of some of Trollope's critics was even harsher towards his frank declaration that he also wrote for money. However, despite his waning popularity, some of Trollope's contemporaries like the Americans Henry James and Julian Hawthorne expressed their appreciation of Trollope's witty and strong painting of reality.

In 1880, Trollope's asthma made him decide to resort to seclusion in a rather rural region named South Harting. He was then an old man with a declining health, yet he carried on writing more novels, the last of which was the never-finished *The Landleaguers*.

In September 1882, he returned to London and died there on December 6th following a sudden stroke.

Anthony Trollope – A Bibliography

Single Novels
The Macdermots of Ballycloran (1847)
The Kellys and the O'Kellys (1848)
La Vendée: An Historical Romance (1850)
The Three Clerks (1858)
The Bertrams (1859)
Castle Richmond (1860)
Orley Farm (1862)
The Struggles of Brown, Jones & Robinson (1862)
Rachel Ray (1863)
Miss Mackenzie (1865)
The Belton Estate (1866)
The Claverings (1867)
Nina Balatka (1867)
Linda Tressel (1868)
He Knew He Was Right (1869)
The Vicar of Bullhampton (1870)
Sir Harry Hotspur of Humblethwaite (1871)
Ralph the Heir (1871)
The Golden Lion of Granpère (1872)
Harry Heathcote of Gangoil (1874)
Lady Anna (1874)

The Way We Live Now (1875)
The American Senator (1877)
Is He Popenjoy? (1878)
John Caldigate (1879)
An Eye for an Eye (1879)
Cousin Henry (1879)
Ayala's Angel (1881)
Doctor Wortle's School (1881)
The Fixed Period (1882)
Kept in the Dark (1882)
Marion Fay (1882)
Mr. Scarborough's Family (1883)
The Landleaguers (1883)
An Old Man's Love (1884)

Chronicles of Barsetshire
The Warden (1855)
Barchester Towers (1857)
Doctor Thorne (1858)
Framley Parsonage (1861)
The Small House at Allington (1864)
The Last Chronicle of Barset (1867)

Palliser novels
Can You Forgive Her? (1865)
Phineas Finn (1869)
The Eustace Diamonds (1873)
Phineas Redux (1874)
The Prime Minister (1876)
The Duke's Children (1880)

Short stories
Tales of All Countries--1st Series (1861)
Tales of All Countries--2nd Series (1863)
Gentle Euphemia (1866)
Katchen's Caprices" (1866)
Lotta Schmidt & Other Stories (1867)
An Editor's Tales (1870)
Christmas at Kirkby Cottage" (1870)
Never, Never -- Never, Never (1875)
Catherine Carmichael (1878)
Why Frau Frohmann Raised Her Prices and other Stories (1882)
The Two Heroines of Plumpington (1882)
Not If I Know It"

Non-fiction
The West Indies and the Spanish Main (1859)
North America (1862)
Hunting Sketches (1865)
Travelling Sketches (1866)
Clergymen of the Church of England (1866)

On English Prose Fiction as a Rational Amusement (1869)
The Commentaries of Caesar (1870)
Australia and New Zealand (1873)
New South Wales & Queensland (1874)
South Africa (1878)
How the 'Mastiffs' Went to Iceland (1878)
Iceland (1878)
Thackeray (1879)
Life of Cicero (1880)
Lord Palmerston (1882)
An Autobiography (1883)
London Tradesmen (1927)
The New Zealander (1972)

Plays
Did He Steal It? (1869)
The Noble Jilt (1923)